WALKING IN THE
FIRE

WALKING IN THE
FIRE

A LOVE STORY

Susan Erhard

XULON PRESS ELITE

Xulon Press Elite
2301 Lucien Way #415
Maitland, FL 32751
407.339.4217
www.xulonpress.com

Memoirs of My Journey with God
© 2020 by Susan Erhard

Unless otherwise indicated, Scripture quotations taken from the King James Version (KJV)–*public domain.*

Printed in the United States of America.

ISBN-13: 978-1-6312-9309-2

DEDICATION

This book is dedicated to my four children who are the blessings of my life. It is also dedicated to my eleven grandchildren who may also find joy in discovering their roots and the retelling of some of the family stories.

ACKNOWLEDGMENTS

I would like to thank Carol for her listening ear as this book took form. A thank you to Janie who typed it, Brian who found me a place to begin publishing and Cindy who was able to send it to be edited. To Shirley who is always there for me. You are loved!

TABLE OF CONTENTS

The Beginning - An Ordinary Day xi

Looking Back

1963 – Welcome to the Real World 1

Now a Wife and Married Life!. 6

No Money, Honey…Just Love. 13

Pride Goes Before…It All 17

Twelve Conclusions I Have Pondered 20

Mother, Help! 22

Life Changes Ahead. 25

Motherhood, There Is No Way Back
    to Before. 27

God Leads Forward. 36

Friends 39

A Place to Call Home 43

Motherhood and Laughter. 46

Another Move 50

The Anxieties of the Vanity 56

God Looked Me Straight in the Eye
    and Winked!. 58

Tradition Is the Keystone. 63

Each New Day. 66

The Surgery 70

The Days of Death 72

My Mother's Death 78

A Rocking Chair of Love 81

A Cup of Tea Please 85

Your Only Choice Is Forwards 87

Now You See Me, Then You Don't. 90

The Cross. 92

Town Celebrations. 97

Holidays 100

The Bucket List 103

The Dance 106

It Is a Long Journey. 108

Our Family Circle – A Letter to My
    Children 112

A Proud American! 115

The Rescue! 119

Final Word 126

About the Author 129

The Beginning

AN ORDINARY DAY

It was just an ordinary day. We had scheduled an appointment to see a new physician, a neurologist, about the back pain and assorted other symptoms my husband, Denny, was having. His regular doctor was unable to diagnose his condition and had sent him to a specialist. Denny was anticipating several revealing health tests and asked me, with my nursing background, to accompany him into the examining room to interpret the medical discussions that were about to occur. He was told to change into a hospital gown.

The physician came into the room and asked Denny to walk across the room. He asked him to flex his hands and smile. He then told him to get dressed.

Denny looked at me and said, "Uh-oh, that's not good. What happened to the electronic exam I was to have?"

The neurologist left the room and returned shortly, looking anxious. It was only one day in our life, but it changed our lives forever!

The change began immediately with the neurologist's next few words, "I'm pretty sure you have

Parkinson's Disease! It is a difficult disease to diagnose. There is no definitive test. It is a disease defined by the elimination of other diseases for which there are tests. However, when I was a young neurologist, I was unable to diagnose my grandfather with the disease. My grandmother has never let me forget it! Therefore, I am now somewhat of an expert at diagnosing Parkinson's Disease."

Denny was only fifty-eight years old and we still had the last of our four children in college. This certainly was not in the plans for our lives! I did not want to believe the doctor's conclusions.

We went home in silence, not knowing what to say to each other. I did not sleep that night or the next night. Instead, I sat at my desk and recorded the following in my diary.

Dear Diary,

Funny, as I look outside into the dark night, nothing has changed in the view from my family room window. Yet, everything has changed. The last time I felt this way was when my brother, David, died. People called then and brought food, all kinds of food. I remember thinking that was a strange thing to do. Who even feels like eating when your brother has died? But later, I understood. People who visited you from far-away places needed to eat. We lived in a small rural community with no available fast-food restaurants. Food was a considerate gift! I think I served a thousand sandwiches in those three days. At least it felt like a thousand.

Today, no one brought sandwich ingredients. No one called. It is silent! Denny did not go to work yesterday or today because he does not know what to say to other people. He is not sure what this will mean for his life.

"Mr. Erhard, I am pretty sure you have Parkinson's Disease," the doctor had said.

He paused and gave us a moment to absorb the statement and then he said, "It probably will not cause your death. It will just make your life difficult!"

Denny and I had looked at each other and wondered what that meant for us. The doctor began to explain, but I am not sure either of us really heard what he was saying. He realized we needed to let the whole thing sink in before we could comprehend anything further and set up another follow-up appointment to further inform us.

As we left his office, he said,
"Things will never be the same again.
You will never sweat the small stuff again!"

Tonight, as I sit here writing out my thoughts, I realize that is not exactly true. I am having trouble sorting through everything coming into my thoughts—big, small, insignificant, and important.

Do we need to find a new home? Our current home sits on the side of a rather steep hill and would be difficult to maintain.

Should Denny retire now so we have quality time together before it ends in an inability to get around without aid! He is my best friend, my lover, and the father of our four children. I love him so much. I cannot think of him in a degenerating disease. Denny is such a kind and good man.

Throughout the day, I struggled with all these thoughts flowing through my mind. I even forgot to make lunch yesterday after we came home from the hospital. I did not make dinner today until way into the evening. Shouldn't someone bring something to eat? It feels like someone died!

Our journey together in life had begun when we were high school sweethearts. We were fully in love with each other, nothing to our names, and a bright hope for the future. We both came from families that loved and honored the Lord. Our roots were small-town "planted" and rather protected from the mayhem of the sixties!

We had already weathered many difficult and life-changing events in our lives. However, contemplating the unknown changes about to occur with such a debilitating disease entering our lives, could become total fear if the Lord does not remain our anchor.

**Even knowing the Lord,
the battle we are facing will be to
stay on the path of faith,
while walking among the flames
that seek to consume us.**

Looking Back

1963 – WELCOME TO THE REAL WORLD

I did not know how unusual and secluded my small town in Central Pennsylvania was until I went away to nursing school in 1963. My entire family was busy moving me into my new room when I noticed my nursing school roommate seemed to be alone. She announced that her parents were divorced, her grandmother had raised her, and there was no one available to help her move, so she had moved in herself.

I was speechless! I never knew anyone whose parents were divorced! Not just divorced from each other, but apparently, in some way, from their daughter as well. I felt so sad for her, but she seemed to take it all in stride. That was just the way it was! Welcome to the real world, Susan, and the beginning of the '60s Cultural Revolution.

Growing up in a small town was not just an experience, it was a privilege.

My neighbors were mostly of the Amish and Mennonite faith and the remainder of townsfolk were aunts, uncles, and first, second, and third cousins. Both sets of grandparents lived practically next door to me. Each pair of grandparents operated one of the two general stores in town. Each child in town was definitely accountable to every other child's parents and they felt free to discipline you as if you were their own. It was a system that worked well in those days! We did not have any town police, but order was still maintained.

I was a little girl in pigtails, who went to a quaint three-room country school with slate chalkboards and oiled floorboards; where learning manners and scripture verses were as important as the ABC's. Grown-ups always had the last say and any disrespect was reported to one's parents immediately. Our playground was the whole town and any place left unattended was fair game for entry. At different times, our hideout, slash, playhouse was an old barn, a tool shed or a chicken house. The chicken house came with a secret escape where the chicken running board exited out the back wall. As I look back, it seems like a segment taken right out of The Walton's TV show.

They were idyllic days and I planned on them lasting forever! Lives were lived very orderly and almost no one moved away from their roots. I planned to go to nursing school and marry my high school sweetheart. I then planned to move back home to that same small town and raise a family.

I Planned, But…

I planned, but real life began for me with a simple phone call shortly after I started nursing school. I was told my brother, David, had been taken to the hospital with grand mal seizures. Tests followed more tests and it was discovered that my brother had a malignant, grapefruit-sized tumor growing in his head. The tumor was removed and time passed. We all believed he was healed, but then the seizures began again. This time, he died in a very short time. My world was feeling very shaky. I had never planned for this kind of thing happening or feeling this kind of grief. I turned to what I had been taught in my childhood for comfort, Jesus. The journey in faith then really began for me.

I began a search to discover how my roots, my faith,
and my family heritage would make me into the woman
whom the Lord had created me to be.

I thought I needed to do something, but what?
The sixties were a time of great unrest. It was popular
in some areas to display billboards that said, "Is God
Dead?" That would never be permitted in the town
where I grew up. God was real and most of us knew
it! But did I really know Him? I committed my life to
Him at an early age. I knew His name, but I did not
know His heart. The death of my brother, the loss of
his presence in my life and believing he was in heaven
made the journey to know the Savior in an intimate
way imperative.

> *I asked myself, "Was all that had taken*
> *place just a random act of God or was it*
> *part of a divine plan to help shape who*
> *I would be in my future?"*

**The journey for an answer to that question had
begun in my life.**

Have you ever wondered if God had a
divine plan for your life?

Now a Wife and Married Life!

I met Denny as a young girl of fourteen. Our individual schools had experienced a jointure and I was selected to go to the new school as part of the blending of the two systems. One day, he came jogging across the outdoor track, stopped in front of me, told me his name, and asked me to the school dance.

I was not impressed with his "ducktail" haircut and bold attitude, so I said, "No."

He laughed. He showed up at the dance and cut into every dance I accepted with someone.

He would ask me during the dance, "Do you like me now?"

I would answer, "No."

After that, he sent notes through my cousin and met my bus every day, walking me to my locker. One day, he was not at the bus stop. The next day he laughed and said several people said I looked for him.

He asked, "Do you like me now?"

I answered, "Yes."

As our relationship continued, he changed his mantra to, "Do you love me now?"

I would answer, "No."

He would say, "Don't worry, you will!"

One day after he turned eighteen, he said he had been praying up on the hill behind his house and God told him not to worry that I would be his wife one day.

Denny and I were engaged while I was just a second-year nursing student. In those conservative days, there were many restrictions while attending nursing school. One unpopular one was a curfew of 7 P.M. during the week and 11 P.M. on weekends. We had house mothers who guarded us like we were their own daughters. There were room checks every night while we were freshmen at seven o'clock. While we were in school, we were under her charge. She took it seriously!

Getting married while in school was not even a consideration for those who wanted to graduate. They believed one could not concentrate on one's studies if they had a husband to consider. Our health instructor, who was single, told us that marital sexual relations caused confusion in one's studies! Sadly, we never got to the basics in those nursing classes.

We were engaged in the summer before my junior year in nursing school. My parents were not happy at the early engagement. They felt sure we would want to marry early. We promised we would not! We broke that promise.

However, once Denny and I were engaged, we began to anticipate our life together. We talked of college for Denny and rationalized that if we were to get married, we could save my wife's military allotment towards his college. We began to plan to elope and not tell anyone of our plans. We planned for me to meet Denny, who was stationed in Maine, in Massachusetts at a family friend's home.

These friends were in their sixties and were happy to comply in the conspiracy. They loved our being in love and promised to keep our secret. However, my mother heard me talking about my trip to New England during my one-week nursing vacation.

She said, "Oh, no….that is too close to Denny's Air Force base and he may not join you without our supervision."

I just said, "Mother, I am going!"

She said, "No, you are not!"

Then just as suddenly, she said, "Susan, are you planning to elope?"

I said, "We have been together since I was fifteen. The Bible says it is better to marry than to burn. Mother, I am about to burn! It is right for us to marry!"

I was usually very compliant, so this was a shocking situation for my parents. Sexual relations before marriage were a big taboo and not looked kindly upon. I was a young Christian girl and knew what the Lord expected of us. Both of our parents had married at an early age. We were determined to marry. My parents got in the car and drove off into the night to talk!

I called Denny in Maine to tell him what had just happened! He wondered if my parents were heading towards Maine. A few hours later, Mother called from a restaurant and said it was my life and she hoped I knew what I was doing! It would be a difficult situation to contain. However, they wanted to come to my wedding and asked if we would please get married at her brother's church in Maryland. We planned a simple wedding and married that winter.

On our wedding day, walking back down the aisle of the church after saying our vows, he asked me if I loved him now.

I answered, "Yes, for forever!"

After marrying my high school sweetheart, my life moved forward with self-consuming diligence. It kept us both busy to pay our bills and focus on getting an education. In the early sixties, it was not uncommon to marry at an early age. Still a small-town girl at heart, I missed the bra-burning revolution and free-love thinking. Its behavior never got to my section of town.

My husband was in the service when we married. There was still a draft and most young men served in some type of military service. My husband volunteered to serve in the Air Force. I was in nurses' training in Harrisburg, Pennsylvania.

All went well until the following winter in my senior year of school. Denny had gotten an early discharge to attend college. I was living part-time as his wife in his college town, just an hour's drive from my school, while appearing single at my school.

The two worlds began to collide when a patient questioned if I was the wife of one of his college students in front of my floor duty instructors.

I lied and said, "No!"

Within a short period of the lie, I became really ill with a ruptured appendix and required surgery. While in the hospital recovering in infection isolation, Denny could not visit because he was not a relative. During that same time, the school had decided to let seniors get married with proper grades and appropriate situations of alternate housing. I was an honor student and Denny was going to school an hour away. I decided I would just go tell the administration about our situation. Since I was an honor student, I was sure if they understood that marriage had not affected my studies at all, there would not be a need for any more deceit.

I was standing at the elevator when the doors opened and a fellow student was sitting on the elevator floor sobbing! She said she was dismissed from school because she had told them she was already married. The administration said there was no excuse for breaking their rules. The dismissal was appropriate! I quickly reconsidered my choices. I would need a new marriage certificate if I was to "come out" of hiding. After much discussion with our hometown pastor, he said he would re-marry us and issue us the needed certificate that the church produced. So, two weeks before our first anniversary, I was married again in my parents' living room.

My mother baked me a second wedding cake.

While I was cutting the cake for the small family gathering, my mother leaned over my shoulder and said, "I hope you have three daughters and they all do this to you!"

When I had my third daughter in a row, I said, "Thanks, Mom!"

Most folks believed that was my wedding day. They sometimes still get the date wrong for celebrating my anniversary. It has been a long time since that first wedding and the telling of those concealing lies. That was not a good way to begin a marriage. There was much emotional suffering without the truth. However, that was fifty years ago, and just think, some people thought it wouldn't last!

Have you experienced emotional suffering
due to concealing lies?

No Money, Honey...Just Love

Denny and I were so restricted in finances that on our first anniversary he did not have enough money to make a long-distance phone call to me. Instead, he purchased a ten-cent thank you card and wrote how thankful he was to have me for his wife. I still have that card in my "drawer of memories" in my dresser under my underwear. I was so happy to be his wife!

When I graduated from nursing school, I moved into our first apartment with a great expectancy of being the ideal wife. Now just what makes an ideal wife? Who knows? Remember, I was a product of all those indoctrinating fifties television shows where mothers wore high heel shoes to vacuum the already-spotlessly clean carpets. However, I was pretty sure doing laundry was a part of my expected duties!

This was only the sixties! I learned many things growing up. I was a really good cook. I cleaned like a whirlwind and I could decorate a home with a wooden barrel and a yard of cloth. However, my mother did the laundry and I did the dishes. I did not learn to do laundry! Our landlord had a set of washers and dryers installed in the hall of the apartment house. Of course, they were maintained by a series of quarters that kept them operating. I was determined to be very frugal on our slim budget. I thought I could save money by hanging our clothes on a line on the roof of the building. I watched the apartment house women hanging their clothes on the roof lines and decided it really was not that difficult. The hard part was finding the lines empty. I actually considered asking one of the ladies her opinion on clothesline propriety, but my pride would not let me.

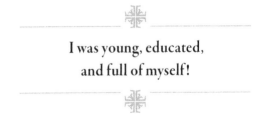

I was young, educated, and full of myself!

The day finally arrived that the lines were clear and the washers as well. I had purchased a laundry basket and clothespins. I climbed out the upstairs window onto the roof of the building with my basket and newly washed garments. I began to hang my clothes in the hot sun. As I hung my clothes on the line, I noticed I had drawn quite a crowd at the various windows of the apartment house. They seemed to be laughing at me, but I wasn't sure. I was wondering why the lines were finally empty and they all had time to watch me out of their apartment windows. I let that thought go as I proceeded to hang the articles just as they came out of the basket—a sock, a shirt, or a pair of underwear. I later learned there is a proper way to hang laundry. For instance, a pair of socks goes with other socks and tidy little "undies" are hung all in a row.

It was becoming quite warm on the roof and I was feeling very uncomfortable with all the spectators. I reached down to pick up my basket only to discover the heat on a tar roof had attached it to the roof. I also discovered that I was attached to the roof as well. I was stuck in the tar up to the top of the soles of my penny loafers. I did not ask for help. I did not look to my right or left, I just marched off the roof in my bare, soon-to-be tar-coated feet! After dark, I sent my husband up to the roof to pry my shoes out of the tar. This was not a money-saving experience since I could not use those shoes ever again, but I did learn at an early stage of my marriage to ask for help when I needed it. Well, I learned to ask for help, sometimes!

How did you learned the importance of
asking for help when you need it?

PRIDE GOES BEFORE...IT ALL

D enny finished college. We built a small home next to my parents on parent-donated land. After moving back to my hometown, I had another experience that should have been remedied by my rooftop experience, but it was not. I still had a lot of pride! The ladies of our church were mostly from the local farming community. The women were great cooks and our church suppers were infamous. I received a telephone call one morning from Frannie, the person in charge of food prep for a church dinner. She appealed to my pride by saying she heard what a good cook I was and would I mind baking five pies for the church dinner. I was stunned! I could bake a pie, but five pies! That would take me all day!

I said, "Yes," and then called my mother in a breathless voice, asking her how I could possibly have gotten myself into such a predicament! The day came to bake, and my mother came and helped me make the pies. Now as a mother of four children, I have often baked five pies, but I will never forget the day

I was first asked to accomplish such a deed and my pride that would not say, "No."

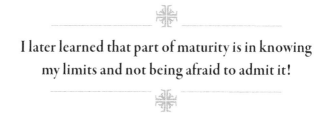

I later learned that part of maturity is in knowing my limits and not being afraid to admit it!

I had a very good friend that was expecting a baby at the same time that I was pregnant with my third child, Carrie. My friend was very dear to me. I was rarely sick during any of my pregnancies, while she was suffering from morning sickness most of those nine months. I was able to take her some meals and help with some minor duties around her home. She had her baby first. I not only delivered after her, but I also went several weeks over my due date. After a visit with her one day, I noticed she began to treat me a little cool.

I called her and asked if I had done something to make her upset with me.

"Yes," she responded. "After you were able to help me so kindly when I was expecting, you refused to let me help you in even the smallest of ways!"

I asked her when I had refused her help! She told me that I had not only refused her offer to prepare me a meal but was seated on the floor and had refused to take her hand. Instead, I had used the arm of the chair to stand. I remembered the incident and also recalled that I was embarrassed that I had gotten so large with child that I thought that I just might pull her down to the floor with me. As I evaluated my behavior further, I realized I could be quite prideful and did often refuse help if it made me look weak. It was difficult to be challenged by a friend, but I did begin to learn to be more sensitive to the sharing needs of others.

**I also confess I was afraid that
pride could literally go before a fall!**

Pause for Reflection...

Does your pride cause you to refuse help if you think it makes you look weak?

Twelve Conclusions I
Have Pondered

W hat have I learned over the years of living and getting a view from the far side of the hill? It seems that I have learned so much that there would not be any more to learn, but that is just not true. Every day brings a new opportunity to learn and grow. Unlike that young woman who approached that clothesline with determination and pride, I hope I have evolved into a woman that can enjoy a new challenge and a new discovery.

Some of the things I have learned are:

1. Never believe you know it all. There is always someone with another bit of information to make the problem clearer.
2. Family is important. Do not take them for granted.
3. Learn from your mistakes and try again. Success may be just one more try away.

4. Forgiveness to others and yourself in life is essential.
5. Friends make the journey in life sweeter and more interesting.
6. Children do grow up; enjoy those years that they are growing.
7. Grandkids are the reward of growing old.
8. Take time to love some part of each day. Today is all you may have left to love.
9. Learn from harms that are committed against you, so that you will not hurt another in the same way.
10. Teach your children that it is always right to do the right thing. Follow your own advice!
11. Laughter hurts less than tears, but sometimes tears are necessary.
12. God is in charge of everything in my life. Without Him, I would have no joy or peace.

Pause for Reflection...

Which of the above things that I have learned is helping you the most in your life's journey right now?

MOTHER, HELP!

My mother taught me when I was still a preteen that mistakes can be steppingstones. I was learning to sew a skirt for a 4H Club competition. I had almost completed the skirt when I was trimming it for leftover threads. I inadvertently cut a small hole in the front of the skirt just below the waistband. I was hysterical with tears as I saw my whole summer's project destroyed.

My mother looked calmly at the skirt and asked me what design I saw in the fabric. I told her that it was made up of small gold crowns on a deep red fabric. She asked me if I thought I could make a pocket out of the fabric that would look like the crown design of the fabric. I thought for a minute and then cut a crown pocket out of the material. She showed me how to sew the seam around the crown shape and then to turn it inside out to form the pocket. My mother then went and got two gold buttons, jewel-like, and helped me attach the pocket to the skirt over the clipped area on the skirt. It looked fabulous! Later that summer, when I went before the judges, they were very complimentary for the creative pocket. I got a blue ribbon for my project.

Some mistakes are steppingstones!

I was to learn the same lessons thirty years later when my husband was entertaining his whole staff for a Christmas luncheon that I was preparing. I had purchased a ham at a grocery store that I rarely frequented. I later learned that important events require reliable resources. I was baking the ham to slice for the main course of the luncheon. I had all of the remaining of the food was prepared when the ham was ready to be sliced. My mother was visiting me at the time and was busy putting the food on the buffet table.

When I sliced the ham, to my horror, there was a huge strip of fat running through the whole ham. It not only looked terrible, but it was also now no longer enough meat to serve the crowd of people I was about to entertain! My mother asked what other meat I had in the house that would be compatible with the ham and easily prepared. I did not think I had anything!

"All I have is the sausage for tomorrow's breakfast," I said.

She quickly took the sausage and began to brown it on the stove. She told me to make a barbecue sauce, while she cut the remainder of the usable ham off the bone. Gently, I folded the ham and sausage into the sauce. I placed it on a huge platter with sliced oranges and apples around the platter. It looked great, tasted wonderful, and was the hit of the buffet! Sometimes mistakes are steppingstones.

The BIG LESSON is,
"Keep calm, think rationally,
and use the resources around you,"
especially if one of them is your MOTHER!
Thank you, my sweet Mama.

Pause for Reflection...

Has this section helped you to begin to view mistakes as steppingstones and to use the resources around you?

Have you thanked your mother today for the valuable resource she has been in your life?

LIFE CHANGES AHEAD

After serving in the Air Force, Denny went on to college and earned a master's degree. He was the first person in his family to graduate from college. His father was the first to graduate from high school in his family. His father literally walked six miles to attend school in town, if he missed the occasional milk wagon ride. His father's dad was an orphan. The orphanage supervisors named him George Washington Erhard. My husband said he did not believe that was his name until he saw it on his grandfather's tombstone.

Denny's Dad was about 120 pounds.

His Dad's friend said, "He was the biggest little man he ever knew."

When Denny received his master's degree, his father wanted to know what that was "good for."

He said he was, "So proud of Denny for all that book learning!"

Denny's degree was in guidance counseling, which led him to a career in management for the Pennsylvania Department of Corrections.

However, as Denny continued to receive job promotions, his Dad seriously asked him if he had trouble keeping a job! It was a new world to his Dad's hard-labor life.

The struggle to become educated was difficult, but we had prayed and believed we were in God's plan for our lives. I worked in the operating room of the local hospital until we started our family.

Pause for Reflection...

How has your family heritage affected your choices in life, especially in the area of education and employment?

MOTHERHOOD, THERE IS NO WAY BACK TO BEFORE

I was crazy in love with my husband and anxious to start a family. I came from a happy family-circle environment. Children were always a part of the discussions for the future of our marriage. I had no real idea of what was about to happen to my life as children became a part of it! Does anyone? The Lord was about to stretch my faith. We were anxious to have children be a part of our marriage. What I was not to discover until years later was, "Once a mother always a mother!"

I thought you raised your children and then they were adults and went out on their own. Now in theory that is what happens. However, a mother's heart is forever tied into the heart of her children, and their footsteps on the porch are discernible to her ears, whether it is midnight or two o'clock in the afternoon. My child's voice tenor on the telephone sends me a clear message before a single sentence is spoken.

Motherhood is forever!

Our daughter Carla was conceived while Denny was still in college. We were so excited about having her as a part of our new family. She did not arrive until after he had graduated, and we had moved back to our hometown. Everything seemed perfect. Just a short time later, she was joined in our family by her sister Katrina. It was almost five years later that Carrie was born, and then a surprising five years later that David became a part of our completed family. When our oldest child started college, our youngest child started kindergarten. Later, we discovered the spread in the ages of our children meant that we would have college tuition bills for seventeen years. There was one year we had a break, but we had two of the three daughters get married that year. College tuition was less expensive than that year!

In the early years of our marriage, I had a part-time nursing job as a nighttime supervisor at a local retirement home. I was at work one evening when I received a phone call from my husband. He told me that our second daughter, Katrina, had a severe seizure and my parents had taken her to the local hospital which was 18 miles away.

He did not think she was breathing when they left for the hospital and in a small voice he said, "I think she is dead."

I had no relief nurse on duty that night and therefore could not leave the retirement village unsupervised. I was near panic but managed a brief prayer. The main entrance to the home opened just as I finished praying and the daytime supervisor walked through the door. She had left her purse behind by mistake and had just realized it as she was preparing for bed. Her husband chose to drive her to the home rather than have her go alone. Just what I needed someone to relieve me and a driver to take me to the hospital, help arrived.

My husband told me the details of what had happened at home. He had put our six-month-old daughter to bed. He usually went downstairs to watch television, but this night he decided to write a letter to the local newspaper over an issue he wished to address. While composing his letter, he heard a loud rhythmic banging on the wall in the children's room. When he went to check on the sound, he discovered she was having seizures.

We lived far away from ambulance service and there was no 911 in those days. He still had our two-year-old daughter in bed. He raced Katrina next door to my parents, they jumped in their car and raced to the local emergency room. Mother performed mouth-to-mouth resuscitation as she had just seen on television. Our two-year-old, Carla, in the meantime, had climbed out of bed and left the house wandering in the grass between the homes, in the dark. Friends of ours from our Bible study had decided to take a very late-night walk and discovered our daughter walking alone in the grass. They quickly assessed the situation and took Carla home with them for the night. All we had need of was provided for us in the midst of the storm.

When we arrived at the hospital, she had already begun to breathe on her own but was then admitted to the pediatric unit. The doctors were not aware of what was causing her illness. We prayed and, of course, were concerned that the dreaded seizures that my brother had suffered were to be inflicted on our daughter. The first day she was in the hospital, I just sat by her crib and prayed. Late into the second day, she broke out in a rash that covered her entire body. She had reacted to her immunization shot for the measles by contracting them herself. There was a quick effort made to get her out of the hospital and home. They did not want measles spread over the pediatric unit.

Not for the last time, but for the first, I had begun to realize that to have a child meant to constantly turn that child back to the Lord for His care and providence.

Each child was but a loan from the Lord,
entrusted to our earthly care.

The faith anchor grew stronger as I realized I was not in this life alone. God went ever before me, opening and closing doors and providing solutions, sometimes before I even asked!

I am the mother of four children! I sometimes cannot believe that is true. I always envisioned a tidy family of four. If you think about it, there are very few places in public that easily accommodate a family of six. We went directly from the family station wagon to the family minivan, a great invention. Restaurant booths were a tight fit and usually required an extra booth. An extra booth usually meant trouble. Children are very creative when left alone. Does anyone still remember the seventies when hairpieces and wigs were popular? Our daughter, Katrina, was fascinated with wigs.

Once a month, we took the children out for Sunday lunch. We were busily studying the menu when the lady in the booth behind Katrina left out a loud squeal. Katrina had pulled the lady's red-haired wig off her pin-curled head. My husband, who is usually cool in most situations, succinctly placed the lady's wig back on the top of her head like a bird's nest waiting for its first egg deposits. It was very embarrassing but also funny.

One cannot raise children without a certain amount of embarrassing moments. This is just one of many. Our eldest daughter, Carla, was three. I was in a hurry to retrieve the morning newspaper and noticed the delivery person had thrown it on the patio instead of the porch. I thought I could make a quick trip in and out of the house within a few moments. When I stepped onto the porch, I heard the door being slammed shut! This would not be such a terror-filled event except I was wearing the brief outfit of black baby doll pajamas.

I yelled to Carla to open the door immediately. She shook her head and said that I was angry with her. I tried convincing her that I just wanted her to let me back in the house! After several failed attempts of getting her to do my bidding, I realized I was less dressed than more dressed and it was about to become embarrassing. I checked the window locks and discovered the only one open was the very small and high-located bathroom window. With no other choice, I scaled the siding of the ranch house and climbed in the window. My telephone was already ringing when I got into the house. My dad was calling to tell me several neighbors had called him to say I was undressed and climbing in a window.

When I return to my hometown, I occasionally meet someone who still enjoys a laugh at my expense over that recalled memory!

There are always events to remind you as a parent that life is very fragile and should be held as a precious treasure each day. Our daughter, Carrie, was a beautiful child. Her Grandmother Erhard was always saying how much she looked like her daughter, Barbie, who died as a toddler of epiglottis (essentially suffocating). That was a little fear tickler that would play around in my brain when I felt overly protective of her lively personality and beauty. She was particularly susceptible to croup and we spent many hours with her in the steam of the shower.

One night she was coughing deeply and then I heard her stop in mid cough. I rushed over to her room and discovered she was no longer breathing. I picked her up in my arms while trying to breathe in her mouth. My husband called a neighbor to come over to watch the other children while we raced to the car to take her to the hospital. We now lived only a few miles from the emergency room. While I was holding her, the evil fears in my head were claiming her as dead. I was praying out loud claiming that only Jesus had the power to take her life. Carrie belonged to Him. The decision for life or death was Jesus'.

The emergency room was in a small-town hospital that was only staffed by a nurse. They had to call a physician. It was two o'clock in the morning. Carrie was lying on the stretcher gasping in small gurgles. She had epiglottis. At the moment of crisis in her life, a young doctor came walking through the ER. He said he was visiting a friend who was in the hospital on his way from Pittsburgh Hospital to Johns Hopkins'.

He was a specialist in ear, nose, and throat. He rapidly assessed the situation and asked me if I trusted him. He said he could save her life. I had been praying for such a miracle, but the nurse yelled we did not even know this man and why would we do anything he said! She was preparing to do a tracheotomy *(cut an air hole in her throat). He looked at me and I gave him permission to treat her. He quickly initiated a non-surgical procedure that has since become the standard procedure of treatment for this disease. He was about to lecture on this procedure in the Baltimore hospital. I had given this child life through conception, but only God had her days numbered on this earth.

**I often thank the Lord for the faith He gave me
in proportion to what He was allowing in our lives.**

While we loved our children dearly, we looked forward to the time that we would have our children educated and we would be free to travel and explore the world. We had just spent the last eighteen years sending an educational check off to one university or another, but we were now approaching those much-anticipated days of retirement. Our fourth child was in his fourth year of college.

Pause for Reflection...

Give an example of where the Lord has given you faith in proportion to what He was allowing your life.

GOD LEADS FORWARD

We had our four children during the years when Denny's career required moving our family to various homes located on the grounds throughout the corrections system. This was a very confusing time for me. I was concerned for his safety. We had planned a secure teaching job for him after college, while we lived surrounded by friends and family as we raised our children.

When he was offered a new promotion, a whole new life was about to begin for us. He was asked to relocate to a home on the prison property with the acceptance of this new administrative position. I now had to lay all my fears before the Lord! He had cared for my husband as he worked in the prison, but could he also care for us as we raised our children on prison property? The answer, of course, was "Yes!" I, however, needed to receive that peace in my heart and mind.

We sold that sweet home we built in our secure hometown and began an adventure that would not end for twenty-nine years in a career in corrections. We made new friends and discovered that many other people loved the Lord. Even though we did not always agree on the interpretation of some of the scriptures, we found common ground in the sacrificial love of our Savior and the grace He offered in our salvation. We grew in our love for the Lord and we began making life-long friends.

We had belonged to a Bible study in our hometown and even though we had moved away from the area, it was close enough to travel back for Bible study and other events. Those friends encouraged us to search for new opportunities to start another group in our new location. I was not sure how that would happen. Frankly, we had little desire to go to another Bible Study. We were not sure we knew enough to have a study at our home. However, with their encouragement and prayers, we began to also pray.

I was invited to a luncheon and sat with a group of women who were each there alone. We began to talk about our situations and I said that my Bible study was praying we would find new people with a heart to start a new study. Each woman responded that she and her husband were probably interested in coming to my house to be a part of a new study. WOW! I could hardly believe my ears. Each couple arrived at our home to begin a new study group.

We grew so much during this time in scripture knowledge, in friendships, and even more important, in love and faith of the Lord. Years passed and once more my husband was offered a job. This time it was not in the area and this time we were not really asked; we were told to move or resign. There were many changes taking place in the Department of Corrections and we were caught in the middle of the reorganization. It was not a move we desired, but it was a move we made!

I was losing my friends and I did not want to move. However, the decision was made for Denny to move on ahead of the family while I settled our current situation and located new housing for us.

Pause for Reflection...

Have you been caught in the middle of circumstances beyond your control, but God assured you He was still in control?

FRIENDS

I know that friends have made me stronger, smarter, and my life more challenging. Growing up in the country provides the best formula for making friends! We had no local movie houses, no video games, and no staffed educational or entertainment facilities. We were on our own to entertain and develop our social lives. I learned at an early age that friends were everything! My best friend lived next door. As an adult, I now realize that her mother should be nominated for sainthood. Her mother worked out of the home. My mother was a postmaster at the local post office and available to me at a moment's notice, which did leave me free to be mostly in other children's home spaces to play. We rarely played indoors; outdoors was the designated children's play area.

Our neighbors had a barn behind their home. One of the sections was designated to collect clothing for charitable donations. We were forbidden to play in that area. However, it was our favorite place to play dress-up! We would try on all the local give-away dresses and try to imagine or guess who gave it to the poor people of the world.

One day, we were thrilled to find an entire box of ladies' underwear. They were of a substantial size. One particular size was so substantial that we were able to each get in a separate leg of the boxer panties and one side each of a cotton bra. We stuffed the rocket pointed bra for a realistic look and took off to the local mercantile to purchase some penny candy!

Someone called home! This was not good for us! On the way home from the store, we were met by my friend's mother coming towards us with wrath pasted on her face. I tried, unsuccessfully, to unhook myself from the bra and run. She was faster and in a second I was being carried, mid-air, by the substantial garment straps towards a home deposit. As I told you before, all parents felt free to discipline and would command lockouts for their properties as the offense demanded. I received a two-week, cannot-come-over punishment for that performance. I was a creative child. Not seeing your friend for two weeks was a huge punishment.

My cousin, Nancy, lived across the field and was another source of a great friendship. There was only four months difference in ages and we shared much of the same gene pool. We also got into situations that were boredom inspired. She had a donkey named Mose. He lived up to his domestic history and was quite stubborn. We would ride him around town and wave at everyone, hoping to impress them with the new mobility that donkey travel gave us.

At one point, he decided he wanted to go home, while Nancy pulled the reins in the opposite direction. He promptly went into an impressively kept, Amish neighbor's garden. Now Amish gardens are not only sources of great pride for the planter, but a source of food for the entire family. Mose would not budge when prompted but laid down in the well-kept garden. He destroyed the garden's order. Trying to solve the problem ourselves was not working.

True to form someone called her home. As my aunt approached the mutilated scene, I took off for home, leaving Nancy to suffer the consequences. After all, Mose was her donkey (so much for the loyalty of a friendship). I was not always what I should have been to a friend! I had no sisters, but in life, Nancy has become the closest to being like one. All of our lives we have shared family history and family events. Regular telephone calls are a standard and always when most needed.

**Through the years, friends have made
the best of times sweeter
and the difficult times bearable.**

Denny and I have moved so many times that the best of those moves were new friends and the worst of those times were the loss of fellowship of those friends. Heaven and restoration of those fellowships will be wonderful.

Pause for Reflection...

How have friends impacted your
life's journey?

A Place to Call Home

Denny had moved into temporary quarters while I was house searching. This was in 1979 when the housing market went crazy with 20 percent interest rates and money was rarely available to borrow at the banks. I was bitter at the loss of control of our lives; my husband was feeling the same way. We knew we needed to pray and confess our bitterness and with difficulty we did.

While my husband and I were living in different places, the Holy Spirit visited each of us to give us His peace and assurance that we were not alone; that He would go with us to the ends of the earth. We waited for His direction. It came with a phone call from our Realtor who told us there was a fabulous deal on a new home. If we had the cash to put down on the property, the builder would hold the loan at a reasonable rate. Remember, we had moved into a prison property years before, so we did have liquid funds. The Lord provided once more and it was even more than we had imagined! We even had an extra bedroom in our new house or did we?

I had started back to college to get a degree in family counseling. Denny and I had long-range plans to open a family counseling service in our hometown area. I loved school and was excited about my studies. Several months into the new school year, I became really sick. I believed I had the flu. I battled symptoms for several weeks. I went to the doctor and he said he was going to run a pregnancy test.

I said, "Oh, I couldn't be pregnant!"

He came back into the room and said, "Oh, but you are pregnant! The test doesn't lie!"

Our lives were about to change again! Pregnancy was not part of my plans! Could it part of God's?

One would think that after these experiences, I would never question God's leading in my life again. He was the great provider and He continued to be through some difficult financial times. We were once more in a church and small group fellowship that we loved. I was sure this was the place God had for us to raise our children and be a part of an expanding church. I thought I understood why God had brought us through those difficult times. I felt secure.

Pause for Reflection...

How has God shown you He is your provider no matter what the circumstances you are facing on your life's journey?

MOTHERHOOD AND LAUGHTER

(Article by Sue Erhard taken from "Light Shine," New Covenant
Fellowship, Shiremanstown, PA, June 7, 1981)

A year has passed since last Mother's Day and I have become the mother of another little baby. It is different this time. After three girls, I now have a little boy. Yet, the joy of motherhood is very much the same. I feel the warmth of his head as he struggles to snuggle deeper into my shoulder. His little hands clasp for security to my neck. I hear his giggle of glee when I enter his room and I see him peeking above the bumper pad in his crib. I am awakened by the loud cries of hunger at 5 A.M. or sometimes 6 A.M., but rarely 7 A.M. Does anyone else want to look around at the world at 5 A.M.? Is this really my child? I can't think that early, but he is at his prime!

Motherhood, I am blessed! I recently wrote home to my mother. I told her that I finally understood after all years (certainly not in high school) what the great author meant when he wrote these words: "These are the best of times: these are the worst of times."

I start each day with enthusiasm and purpose to make it through until 10 P.M. Then begins a day filled with piano lessons, trips to the orthodontist/dentist/pediatrician for checkups, five bottles, a kiss over a bumped head, and a band-aid for a skinned knee. (Carrie tells everyone that I am a nurse, so I regularly put band-aids on all the neighborhood children.) I prepare meals, entertain guests of all ages, clean, cook, wash, iron (as little as possible), love, pray a lot, and listen to the tales of my kindergarten, fifth grade, and seventh-grade girls. I delight in their conversation with me (doing the dishes is still a great way to communicate). My daughters are delightful young ladies with budding insights into humanity and good versus evil. I love them.

Each child is still a treasure not completely explored or realized. I am blessed and sometimes exhausted and drained. Without the Lord, I would be a complete failure. Only after I became a mother did I fully realize the value of my mother's love, insight, patience, endurance, and firmness (fully supported by my father).

When I was in the early stages of my last pregnancy, I struggled with God's plan to bless us once again with a new baby. I had started college classes to compliment my certificate as a registered nurse. I loved studying. Our youngest was ready to start school so I had the extra time I needed. The plans

I made were inspired by God—at least they were to that point. I just did not see His ending to the story or should I say the beginning to the overall plan.

I prayed a lot and sought His peace. I dug deep into the Scriptures. Then one beautiful day, He showed me Psalm 127:3, "For children are a heritage from the Lord; and the fruit of the womb is His reward."

"What is a 'heritage,' Lord?" I asked.

He gave me the understanding that our children are His inheritance that neither dust nor rust can corrupt. It is a true inheritance—one I can take with me.

This Mother's Day, thanks to the Lord and my beloved husband, I am blessed times four. After David's birth, a dear friend from South Carolina gave me a cross-stitch picture that reads: "God must have loved Erhards—He made so many of them."

Thank You, Lord! I am truly blessed in Your love. Next year, my friend who is also the mother of four children, said that she will send me another picture. This one will have a mother hen with her four baby chicks sitting on her and around her. It will read, "Help me Lord to endure all my blessings."

Thank you, Lord. You are good! And, the gift of laughter helps a lot! *(end of article)*

Did you thank the Lord today for the
inheritance He has blessed you with?

ANOTHER MOVE

Ajob-related promotion my husband expected to get was given to another man. He was asked to move to another area of the state and open a new prison. I was stunned! Years before when there was a rumor we could be moved out of the area to a small state-owned home in the northwest, our growing family would not fit into the small accommodations. I prayed for adequate housing for our large family, "That is all I ask. I will live anywhere if it is just large enough, Lord!" We were able to decline that job offer.

Working in corrections was a lot like being in the military. Status was maintained by job degrees of authority. He would not be able to decline this job if Denny wanted to continue to work in corrections. When we visited the property where my husband was to work, it was isolated and had been abandoned for over ten years. I was not happy about its appearance. As we drove around the prison property, we came to the house that we were expected to live in. It was dark, abandoned, and **huge**! I was reminded of the prayer that I had prayed to the Lord. The size was not an issue. It was over 6,000 square feet. I knew I was going to live in that house! Six months later, our family of six moved onto that prison property.

I thought I had done my duty by moving to a place I did not want to live. I was doing what God wanted and I was honoring my husband by supporting his decision and career. I **believed** I deserved a reward for doing what was the right thing!

Instead, five months later, I was not prepared for what a car accident could do to my life and the lives of my family. I had been teaching women's Bible studies for over ten years and I had never been challenged by physical adversity. I had rarely taken an aspirin, let alone major medication to get through my day. Our son, David, was only five years old and now I had trouble caring for him. I was used to leading others and now I could barely care for my own world.

The man who hit me while I was stopped at a red light claimed I put the car in reverse and hit him. I was unconscious for several hours and relocated by ambulance from the emergency room of one hospital to a trauma unit in another hospital. They told my husband I had a broken neck. I had no feeling in my hands or feet! Everyone in my world began praying for me. I was in excruciating pain when I came in and out of consciousness. I'd had several x-rays in the emergency room.

When I arrived at the trauma unit, they wanted their own x-rays. The new films showed the original break in the neck bones were now minute live fractures. I believe I was healed of a future that might have placed me in a wheelchair! However, recovery was years away! I had problems with my speech, my walking, and migraine headaches were a constant companion for over three years. I could not drive a car due to my injuries and my other health issues led me to several falls that caused me to break my ankle and then to re-fracture my skull! It was, at that time, the most difficult time of my life! I missed my friends and I felt isolated and unable to drive or connect with any new people we had met during our short time living at the prison property.

Weeks passed, I found myself in a depression that I had never experienced before. I pleaded with the Lord for healing and then for some sign that He actually knew that I was located in this remote place with not even a radio or television connection. Our children were having a difficult time adjusting to their new schools and isolated environment. On top of that, I was not recovering from painful headaches. I felt sorry for myself! I was frightened!

I was praying in tears one morning for God's intervention, challenging the Lord to reveal Himself in my day! He seemed absent and I was angry and felt alone. I threw my Bible and it slid off the table. I told God I was not going to tell anyone about Him as it seemed He had deserted me. Suddenly, there was a knock at the back door. Visitors were very rare at that remote, still-to-be-populated prison property.

Denny had sent a satellite television dish installer to the house to wire the house for radio and TV. My Bible was on the floor. As he passed the table, he reached down, picked up the Bible, and asked me what my favorite passage of scripture was. I looked at him and did not answer; I was having a particularly painful headache and did not expect to discuss the Bible with a man off the street. After all, I had just told God I would be silent as far as He was concerned. He passed back and forth by the table several times while discussing his love for the Lord and His faithfulness to him in his life. He invited us to his home for dinner. He said he would call Denny and set up a date for dinner. Our first contact with someone inviting us into their home for dinner. I was silent.

Later that same morning, there was a knock at the front door and when I answered it, there stood Alice, a lady I had recently met! She said she had picked strawberries that day and was already home when the Lord had directed her to drive the fifteen miles back to my home and give me a box of strawberries. Strawberries are my very favorite fruit and I was speechless at the unfolding events that were occurring in my day.

That was the day I learned just how personal God wanted to be in my life!

Even when I was less faithful, questioning, and undeserving, He wanted me to know He loved me and did indeed know where I lived. He would send His love through people I did not know, but people who were faithful and did His bidding on command. My view of God was greatly expanded as I realized I was not alone and that whatever God would allow in my life, He would also be there to help me through! I also learned that day that God had a real sense of humor. I was the object of His love and humor! I never eat a strawberry that I do not think of the Lord's humor as He sent frightened Alice to a prison property with a box of strawberries just to remind me that He could say through His Spirit, "I know where you live, Susan!"

Did circumstances in your life ever make
you wonder if God knows where you are
and what is happening in your life?

What did He do to prove to you He knew
right where you were and what was going
on in your life?

The Anxieties of the Vanity

When David was born, I discontinued my classes to care for him. The girls were all in school. I needed to find a job to begin saving for our daughters' educations. Remember, we had liquidated all our funds to buy a house. I had attended a rubber bowl party and thought it would be more fun to purchase decorator items on a cash and carry plan. I talked to a friend and she agreed to be my business associate. We started our home show business and it grew to be profitable. My businesses helped to educate our four children while allowing control of my schedule to care for them as they grew into adulthood. Denny's career always had him on call, while my nursing career also required my taking call duty. I switched careers to one that I could own and control. I took small business and management classes at night.

I had a decorator and gift shop for over twenty-four years. I also did the interior design for people's homes and offices. In the early years of childrearing, I was always moving my furniture in different display patterns. I was particularly pleased with a conversation grouping I had placed in the center of our living room. I did not know anyone who had dared to place their sofa in such a manner, so I was anxious to show off a bit (remember the title is vanity). All of my friends placed their sofas against the wall.

Our eldest daughter, who was just a toddler, was thrilled to be able to learn to spell her name. She was only three when she started to write her name. She then found a permanent marker and wrote her name in large 6-inch letters across the exposed back of our new sofa. I never was able to boast of a creative design in my living room again! Until the sofa required new fabric, the sofa was always placed against the wall!

Pause for Reflection...

Read Proverbs 31:30.
What does vanity mean to you?

God Looked Me Straight in the Eye and Winked!

I had many side effects while recovering from the car accident. The time following the car accident was a low point in my life! I had migraines on a regular basis and some problems with a spontaneous numbing of my right arm and leg. This numbing led to other accidents such as a fall down my basement steps which led to a broken foot. My second fall down the church steps resulted in another hospital stay with a second concussion.

Perhaps the most annoying disability was a type of speaking disorder that resulted after the big brain scramble which I had suffered from the brain concussion. I could visualize the word in my head that I wanted to speak like a Rolodex moving madly in my brain. I just had great difficulty getting the word from the Rolodex to the spoken word. I found this limiting disorder to hinder even the simplest of conversations.

I had been living in my new location for over a year and had become a part of the Christian Women's

Organization. However, I was unable to drive myself anywhere due to the side effects of the accident. I was meeting new women who would kindly drive to the prison to pick me up for transport. My accident had in some ways connected me to other women. I was teaching a weekly Bible study and served on the administrative board of the organization.

One day, I was asked by a district representative if I would consider becoming a speaker for Christian Women's Club. I quickly said "no" and promptly left for home, feeling guilty the whole way home. I had not asked if this was something God would have me do, but rather rationalized my speech problem would not allow me to speak to an audience without embarrassing myself. I did, however, commit it to prayer and said if someone else asked me, I would consider submitting a sample tape of my testimony. The next day, another leader asked me to consider auditioning for a speaker's position.

When God had met me in the kitchen of my home with a TV Dish installer and a box of strawberries at my front door, I committed my disability to Him. For one year, He stretched my faith as I reached into the community and church to find places to serve Him. Part of that time, people would drive to the prison and pick me up, since my license had been put on hold! I wanted to hand out a disclaimer to my new friends that this person I had become was not the real me. The real me can walk and talk without any difficulty. I was uncomfortable with who I was after the accident! In the past, I had done some public speaking in women's seminars and retreats. I did not think I would speak publicly until I was healed from the speech disorder.

I prepared my testimony on tape and winced when I heard the lulls that were part of my new voice pattern. I gave it to the district representative, feeling obedient, but positive that she would hear and understand that I could no longer speak publicly. She called me the next day and asked me to be the speaker for the March dinner meeting in a nearby town. She said it is a small group and would give me an opportunity to get involved with the speaker's circle. I was very nervous, but I believed that God would not take me where He would not protect me!

The dinner was held on St. Patrick's Day! In this particular town over a third of the population was Irish. The dinner had swelled from a normal thirty-five guests to well over a hundred! I was introduced, and when I stood to speak, I did not know how to say the first word; I went silent! I then looked at the ladies and told them about my car accident and the resulting speech problem. I asked them to be patient as I gave my testimony. It went well. I did need to pause at times, but I felt peaceful as the Lord gave me the courage to speak.

I was packing up my material when a lady came to me with tears in her eyes. She told me that she was a director of nursing at a popular hospital in the state. She had come home to tell her parents that she was planning to resign her directing position due to a speech problem she had developed after a car accident she had six months before. She related that she was embarrassed by the speech disability and had decided to resign rather than deal with it. She said that after she heard me speak that night, she realized God was calling her to not resign her job. She had committed it to prayer and was shocked to hear me relate the same problem she was having in her life.

I was brought into awe of the Lord when I realized once more that He could use every part and all issues of my life if I was willing to commit them to Him. Gradually my speech improved, but in the meanwhile, I gave my testimony whenever I was asked!

My greatest blessing thus far, certainly, was the night the Lord used my weakness to lead another to His will and comfort!

Will you commit even your weaknesses to
the Lord so He can use you to help another?

Tradition Is the Keystone

I grew up in a family where one could depend on things being the same when you needed them to be! It was comforting to know that supper would be on the table at six o'clock. That when you were four or five or six, someone would tuck you in bed at night and say your prayers with you. You knew you would have a birthday cake on your birthday and colored lights on a Christmas tree at Christmas. You knew someone loved you enough to punish you when you broke the rules and would come and get you when you called, no matter where you were and if they were unhappy with you for what you had done! I knew I was loved! I wanted to give that gift to my children as well!

When I was growing up, we always had hot dogs for Sunday evening supper. Sometimes, we took them on spontaneous summer picnics. If you have hot dogs, you have the beginning of a good picnic! I could always invite a friend to stay for supper on Sunday. I knew there were hot dogs to share!

I supposed one could start out to just make a tradition,
but the ones that seem the strongest are
the ones that evolve out of an event that was
memorable!

I just returned from a traditional event that started
with my daughters seven years ago. Our three daughters have always enjoyed each other's company, and
I have enjoyed their enjoying each other. I decided
to offer them a three-night visit to Williamsburg,
Virginia. They were each able to get the time free
and off we went for a weekend of shopping, eating
at our favorite places, and watching "chick flicks"
(their words, not mine)! It was such a successful
time of relationship renewal that it has continued
to be the highlight of our spring schedules. I have to
applaud the husbands who have cared for "months'
old" babies during this getaway time. Two years ago,
one daddy and a helpmate grandfather took care of
five-month-old twins as well as a four-year-old! I am
so proud of the love they share for each other and the
way they show it!

We have traditional foods we always have on certain holidays. Family favorites must be served. It is
not a good time to try all new recipes. Each of us
in the family will work really hard to spend time

together on special event celebrations. It no longer has to be on the exact day, as marriages and extended family have brought on new traditions for all of us. Loving each other and being concerned for the welfare of each other has been and is the biggest and best tradition we could share with our children. To know that no matter when they call, or where they are, we will always come and get them. Love is like that!

Pause for Reflection...

Choose a happy event and make it a tradition for your family or friends!

EACH NEW DAY

Due to Denny's many years invested in a single retirement system, he could retire after our son completed college. In the meantime, Denny began to develop peculiar health symptoms. He denied them at first. I was concerned with his extreme tiredness, his drooping head, and the unusual way he began to position one side of his body. I began to pray for him over a several month timeframe. We visited some friends whom we had not seen for many months. They expressed great concern over Denny's initial appearance and his state of health. It was their comments that motivated Denny to make that first doctor's appointment.

From that appointment on, Denny's Parkinson's continued to progress. Each new office visit to his neurologist brought comments of a new treatment that involved brain surgery. Apparently, there was a treatment that involved the insertion of a type of brain pacemaker called a Meditronic Implant into one's brain. A battery pack is inserted into one's chest and it is programmed by a computer and a skilled handler.

Denny was reluctant to discuss brain surgery. His doctors continued to tell him he was an excellent candidate for the surgery due to his age and health. One visit to the doctor's office, the doctor called another neurologist into his office for a second opinion. He told him that he should at least meet the surgeon and get his opinion on the success of the surgical procedure.

Denny decided he would meet and discuss the surgery with the surgeon. He was very supportive but insisted we go home and decide on a plan for our lives. The surgery was a serious one and required understanding that no surgery is ever without risk. We prayed and waited. Eventually, Denny decided he would have the surgery. We were both scared and nervous despite our prayers. I did not sleep the night before the surgery. I wrote this prayer instead.

Lord, Tomorrow Is Coming

Tomorrow is there waiting for me. It is now just fifteen hours away. I want it to come because it may bring the culmination, the celebration that I have been praying for along with all of our friends and family. I thought that these times draw us closer to

You, Lord. I feel far away. I worry that in this struggle to let You know what I need to happen tomorrow, I have lost the grace to let You control the outcome. Of course, You will be in control! This whole world is Yours to control. The sun, the moon, the raindrops are all at Your beck and call. Please give me the grace to accept the outcome. It has been such a difficult three years. Our life directions have been declared while I study the décor in various medical facilities. I do not think it is me I am worried about, Lord. What will happen to me if Denny is gone? Perhaps it is me I am worried about, too? When something happens to one's long-time life mate, can one separate where he ends and you begin? I know I am trying to build a case, Lord. Do I sound like Job? He had so much more to bring to You than I, yet, here I am Lord! You have been faithful through other difficult times. I make my mind recall them. You have proven who You are so many times. It is just this has been such a long time of no relief dealing with Parkinson's Disease, prostate cancer, and ruptured discs. I am tired and scared, for tomorrow is coming. This time we are so tired, together. He pulls in one direction while I seem to pull in another.

We are both lonely with unspoken fears that we might lose each other, while we waste precious time doing just that...lose each other. Tomorrow is coming, Lord. Please allow the surgery to go well. But now heal our hearts where we are hiding. Amen.

Pause for Reflection...

As you face trying times, spend time
in prayer knowing your Heavenly
Father hears and knows your heart and
your concerns.

The Surgery

The surgery and recovery room time were over nine hours. Denny had a reaction to the pain medication…every kind that they tried. He was in agony and his right leg flailed madly up and down. He went to intensive care. I was only allowed to stay with him for a few minutes. My daughter Carla went with me to a local hotel. The intensive care nurse said I could call every hour to check on his progress. I called every hour for six hours and I could hear him moaning in the background. I cried and I prayed. His leg was still thrashing, and his pain continued.

At four o'clock in the morning, I woke Carla in sheer exhaustion.

"Please pray for your Dad," I said. "My prayers aren't enough. I am exhausted!"

Carla prayed a simple prayer, "Lord, our parents always called You the Great Physician. They taught me to trust You. Please 'show up' and heal my Dad of that terrible pain and his jumping leg! Amen."

I fell into a deep sleep until eight A.M.

We went to the intensive ward to see how Denny was recovering. He was not there! The nurse told us that the most unusual thing had happened at 4 A.M. Denny suddenly stopped flailing his leg and he said the pain had stopped. They had no explanation! They said they needed his bed for a car accident victim and they had transferred him upstairs to a bed on surgical recovery. We quickly rushed to his room to find him sitting on the side of the bed, eating breakfast and pain-free! The Great Physician had indeed "shown up" as an answer to a young woman's faith!

Pause for Reflection...

Reflect on times God has "shown up" and answered your prayer. Take the time to thank Him today for all those answered prayers.

The Days of Death

I was privileged to know all of my grandparents. Therefore, I was also present at each of their funerals. I was very young when my maternal grandfather died and I can still remember what my grandmother's house smelled like with all the flowers surrounding my grandfather's coffin in her dining room. In those days, one did not use a funeral home, the body was placed in mourning at your home. As I grew older, I eventually lost my other grandparents. I knew great loss with each of their passings. I also retain a wonderful treasure in memories waiting to play like stored cassettes.

As I previously mentioned, my brother, David, died a very untimely death. As young children, David and I shared bedroom space, a playroom, and a sweet younger brother, Jonathan. We were more than brother and sister, we were friends. When David died, I felt an unexplainable emptiness. It was not like losing an older grandparent who had led a full life. This felt unfair! David's death changed my perspective on life. I was charged with a purpose for living, to make my life count!

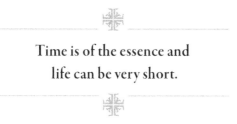

**Time is of the essence and
life can be very short.**

As I write this, my father just died one week ago. His death is fresh and raw. It is a loss like nothing experienced before in my life. He was a huge part of who I am today. I came home from the hospital after he died and sat in the semi-darkness. My mother was silent and refused to let me go home with her. She wanted to be alone. I did not know what to do with my grief! Tears continued to flow down my cheeks as I felt the loss in my soul as I drove home. There was a knock at the door and a recent friend from church came forcefully into the room and perched herself in front of me on the bench. She took my hands in hers as tears slid down her cheeks.

She said, "I have lost both of my parents and I still miss them!"

She was the first person all day to cry with me. I needed those tears of sympathy and the comfort she gave me with those shared tears. We ended our visit in prayer. The scripture says to weep with those who weep and mourn with those who mourn (Romans

12:15). I am so grateful for her faithfulness and her comfort. It gave me courage for the days ahead. It felt like Jesus, Himself had ordered such sweet consolation.

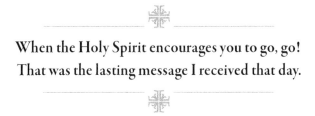

When the Holy Spirit encourages you to go, go!
That was the lasting message I received that day.

I would like to share with you what I was able to share with fellow mourners at my Dad's funeral.

"A Eulogy To My Father At His Funeral"

How does one describe what it was like being the daughter of Carl Updegrove? I have thought so much about this since he died on Tuesday. I cannot talk about my dad without a huge volume of emotion exploding in my soul! I was carved from a gene pool of incredible parents. My daughter Carla said that she could go through the traits she sees in me and singularly assign them to one parent or the other. I know my parents, so I feel incredibly blessed by that compliment. I cannot tell you how many times I have heard from my mother, "You are just like your father!" Now sometimes she was exacerbated with me when she said it!

As I grew up in my home, I learned to love as I watched the unfolding love story that went on between my parents. Dad's love for my mother was perhaps the greatest gift he gave me. I felt secure and expectant in each new day. He gave me hope that tomorrow could be better, even if today was difficult. Dad not only cared for us, but he was also lavish with his gifts. Who could not know him and not have a story to tell about him? He was like an exploding presence in any room he was in. He loved gloriously. Many times, when I was trying to tell someone in one of my Bible studies about the love of our Heavenly Father, I would relate it to their earthly father. I would then discover that they had not been loved like me. Accepting my Heavenly Father's love for me was simple, as I had experienced such personal love already here on earth. Oh, all moments were not blissful; remember I share a lot of his genes. We could both be stubborn, but what Mom many times thought was arguments were just discussions for Dad and me.

I loved him for how he loved other people. I am sure there are people here today who have been recipients of his generosity. Because he felt blessed, he wanted your lives to be easier, too. The food baskets, the paid medical bill, the forgiven rent, or the given folded twenty-dollar bills were common things in my Dad's life. I saw him show compassion, therefore, I learned compassion. On a lighter note, he taught me how to whistle on my long pre-school, school bus rides with him. To this day, I can whistle the Star Spangled Banner which was my graduation whistle! The family could often hear him whistle in a restaurant while he was in the men's room. He seemed to prefer old hymns. He loved life and he loved people. I heard someone said the other day that the whole town is in mourning for my Dad. You have lost an incredible citizen! He certainly loved Allensville and I can tell that the folks who make up Allensville loved him. Thank you for sharing that love with us today. I am privileged to call Carl S. Updegrove my father.

I now concur with what my mother said to me after Dad's funeral. "Heaven is now just that much sweeter of a sounding place to me. It will be a joy to arrive there!" That message was also given to us in scripture: 1 Corinthians 15:55, "O death, where is thy sting? O grave, where is thy victory?"

Pause for Reflection...

When the Holy Spirit encourages you, go and offer sweet consolation in Jesus' name.

MY MOTHER'S DEATH

Just three years later, my mother followed my Dad to heaven. She had spent most of her life with my Dad and missed him tremendously! She gardened in his absence and learned to drive even far distances in a lifestyle she hoped to continue. In the end, a lung tumor and pneumonia took her life.

My mother died and I was not prepared for her death. It has been a year and a half, yet I still have trouble writing about my feelings. When my Dad died three years ago, I became the emotional support of my Mother. I am not sure I realized that until one day I missed calling her and she became upset with me. I had fallen into the practice of calling to check on her each day after Dad's funeral. After several weeks, it was just what I did. I lived over a hundred miles from her. Although my brother lived in the same town as she did, I was her daughter and used to being her emotional caretaker. I loved her!

I am having trouble stabilizing the loss. Perhaps it was because I talked to her daily or was it because there did not feel like there was any closure in our relationship? She was very ill with the shingles the summer she died. One does not expect to die from that infirmity. She did not. It was an undiscovered tumor that grew silently under her left lung masked by the pain of the shingles that was the fatal diagnoses.

My brother was in Mexico on vacation, in the middle of a hurricane, when she died. I had to go immediately and make funeral arrangements after her death. I cried when she died and then I do not remember much after that, emotionally. There was a funeral, guests, and comfort for our children and grandchildren's loss. There was a property to vacate of its contents, attorneys to meet, an auction of goods to plan to pay the taxes, an inherited home to repair and reoccupy. So busy! But there was no closing note left anywhere, only a sterile will with no warmth. I felt abandoned.

It took me a while to understand. Although she had made peace a long time ago with her salvation, she had not really planned on dying either and left without any farewell. My mother, whose protocol was to always say and do the right etiquette for the event, left without an "I love you." She left me some confusing financial matters that would have been better discussed while she was living. I wanted her to have trusted me more to explain more, but it was over. I loved her and missed her. I felt like an orphan.

I have sorted through my parents' life papers and pictures, sometimes feeling like a voyeur. When both parents are gone, it is all there to explore and sort through. Sometimes, I had no timeline to connect the information or photo. It is like, "Who is this and what does this mean?" My mother saved everything. I am still sorting her papers, photos, and books. I have concluded that what was given to me while I was living was full of expression and mostly love and that will have to be enough. I see her in the expressions of our children and even more in my own face as I age. She taught me so many things. She led me to faith in God. She taught me to use the good things you have every day for your family. After all, who is more important than them? She always wanted me to write a book. This is for you, Mom! I love you!

- Susan

Pause for Reflection...

Consider arranging your memories of your childhood and what your parents and grandparents sowed into your life into a book for the next generation.

A Rocking Chair of Love

When I was just a child and I needed to feel loved, I would go across the street to Mom-mom's (my grandmother) and asked to be rocked. She would place me on her lap in a small slipper rocking chair and pat me while she hummed a slightly out of tune, unrecognizable song. I loved to be loved that way. I was sad when I grew too big for her lap. I do not remember her ever telling me she loved me, but I knew she did! I loved her, too! I would sit at her feet when she used her treadle sewing machine and watch her feet rhythmically move the treadle. She made quilt patches out of our old clothes. I have a quilt made by my grandmother's hands, quite a treasure to pass on to my children.

Mom-mom was a woman to be admired. She tended a garden with fervor, she baked pies for resale, and there was always something cooking on one of her two stoves. A quilt was often being quilted in the dining room and the house always smelled of wax and polish. I admired her for her ability to do anything she deemed worthy of her time. She cleaned other people's garden of leftover vegetables and made them into mixed pickles for church or family dinners. I often delivered a pie for her to Grovie, an elderly gentleman who lived in the neighborhood. She would charge him fifteen cents for the pie and give me a nickel for the delivery. This was not a money-making deal for her, I am sure!

I got into some of my worst and most dangerous situations while visiting Mom-mom. My friend Janet and I often played in her attic. There were old coffins stored there from an undertaker she had known. We would "play dead" for scary games on rainy afternoons. Other days, we would be a king and queen on the antique carved church chairs.

One day, when we grew tired of all those games, we pried open the attic windows and stared out into the leaves of the high trees. Janet dared me to jump from the window into the trees, or was it the other way around? I no longer remember. However, I was perched on the frame of the window when Mom-mom came around the side of the house and yelled at me in a horrified voice to stop! I jumped back into the attic with sounds of running feet coming quickly up the steps. She did not believe one waited for your parents to punish you. I immediately received a sound spanking on my bottom as Janet rushed home to the safety of her house. My grandmother called her home as well as mine. I received a duel spanking for that near-death activity.

I not only delivered her pies, I jumped her shrubs while doing a split eagle, I explored her upstairs drawers and closets that smelled like mothballs (I still like that smell), and I sat on the swing with her in the evenings while she pared apples to dry on her kerosene stove in the basement. She ate Sunday dinner with us every Sunday after my grandfather died. After those dinners, she told me stories that made me laugh then and still make me laugh when I remember her telling them.

There was the time she was told that it was not necessary to cut the heads off the chickens to prepare them for eating. She would snap them soundly on the head with a blunt, hard instrument. It was a lot cleaner and easier to accomplish than head chopping! She then proceeded to dip them in hot water and pluck their feathers. If you have not been raised on a farm, chickens do not come in cellophane wrappings. Someone has to prepare the chicken for eating. Grandma said she did the deed and went back into the house to get the remainder of the pans she needed to complete the task. When she came back to the chicken yard, there were the chickens walking about nude as the day they were hatched! Or do they even have a few baby feathers then?

The night she died, I was in nursing school. I was not able to sleep that night and walked over the window as a single dark cloud crossed over the moon. It was midnight. I shivered and rested uneasily that night. At six A.M., I received a call from my mother saying Mom-mom had died during the night. I asked her what time she had died. It was the exact hour I had looked at the moon and cloud. I loved knowing her so much. She taught me that there was always time to stop and show love, no matter how busy your day may be!

**She also taught me self-reliance
for whatever I would choose to do
and that no job is too small to command respect.**

Pause for Reflection...

Always take the time to stop and show love,
no matter how busy your day. Those are
the memories you will leave behind when
you are called to your heavenly home.

A Cup of Tea Please

If my grandmother Updegrove was a typical grandma with a bun in her hair and an apron tied about her neck, Ma was just the opposite! Grandmother Kennedy could be found nestled into a corner of her couch with her legs crossed under her, reading a book or watching a baseball game on television. I always thought calling her "Ma" sounded like backwoods. Backwoods, she was not!

She was the first woman in town to get a college degree. She encouraged me to read. Once she sent me home with a copy of "Peyton Place." It was considered inappropriate for someone my age. My mother was quite upset. Ma believed information was education! I loved to visit her. She was the most modern person I knew. She was the first lady in town to wear pants. I have a picture of her in them. She treated me like I was an adult and loved me as her granddaughter.

Ma taught me to drink tea. She was English, and when I was ten, she gave me a lesson on how to make a proper pot of tea. Boil the water, warm the pot, steep the tea. I would also make cinnamon toast to accompany our tea. I did this until she died. I never learned to drink another hot drink but tea.

My cousin Nancy will call me and say, "I have my cup of tea. Would you like to talk?" Sometimes I will go and get a cup of tea for me.

When my first grandson called me, "Ma," I was determined to change it to grandmother, grandma, or like my friend's name, "Sweety Pie." I tried to correct him to call me Grandma. He ignored me.

One day, I called his house and when he answered the phone, I said, "Hello, this is Grandma."

There was a long silence on the phone and then laughter, "Oh it's you, Ma, you can't fool me!"

Since that day I have been Ma. I now have eleven grandchildren calling me Ma. It sounds just about perfect and always sweet to my ears!

Pause for Reflection...

Cherish those special things your grandparents taught you and thank God for the impact they had on your lives.

Your Only Choice
Is Forwards

It was confirmed by more tests and a physician's second opinion that my husband had Parkinson's Disease. I had my whole life planned from the day I married him over forty-five years ago. As you have read some of these rather light collections of life experiences, there is little preparation for this chapter. That is what a degenerative disease is like. It attacks at the least-expected moment of your life and changes it forever.

We decided we needed to sell our home and move into a more "user-friendly" floor plan. We took a cruise to encourage ourselves that we could persevere towards our travel dreams in even through these difficult circumstances.

Denny quickly discovered that his disease was progressing. He was the Deputy Secretary of Corrections over Pennsylvania State Prisons for the Governor. He decided he could no longer oversee the nine correctional facilities that were his to manage and decided to retire.

In the meantime, he had a routine yearly physical. He had a work associate that continually "bugged" him about just making sure the rest of his physical body was well. Denny had no symptoms of other physical issues. He made the appointment to appease his friend. We were glad he did! It seemed that once again our new life directions were being declared while we waited nervously in the chairs of doctors' offices.

The second declaration was clear, "It's prostate cancer and it will require surgery and radiation treatment."

The third came from a hospital bed when he became totally immobilized. I lay next to Denny in the bed, fearful that the cancer had spread to the bones in his back. Our prayers were more groaning s than words as our spirits did not know how to pray from sheer exhaustion.

The doctor said, "The good news is the cancer has not spread to your back, the bad news is you have several ruptured discs."

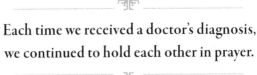

Each time we received a doctor's diagnosis, we continued to hold each other in prayer.

We prayed for a way to continue to deal with our circumstances. In less than three years, our lives had been tossed into turmoil that is particular to illness and a progressive disease. The Parkinson's has interfered with much of his daily activities. The prostate cancer has forced unfamiliar and difficult ways to express intimacy. The ruptured disc has stolen his long hours of comfort gardening. Others now mow our grass.

Pause for Reflection...

Has an unexpected diagnosis caused changes in your life's journey? Remember, your heavenly Father knows where you are and what you need.

Now You See Me,
Then You Don't

One of the most difficult events in the whole ongoing disease scenario is the absence of ongoing friends. Degenerative diseases are never-ending. Things you once could do are no longer possible. If you are the initiator of your circle's "fun and games," it leaves a big hole in the social circle. It is not obvious at first; they just slowly disappear from life! Not everyone, bless their hearts, but enough to create an emptiness that hurts. Denny's speech therapist challenged the loss as not keeping up the good conversation and personality while one's life changes. Denny's voice has been particularly affected by his Parkinson's Disease. Sometimes it is difficult to understand him. This is not uncommon in this disease. What the therapist challenged may be true, however, I thought, can one expect a little more from people who ate regularly in your home and prayed weekly at your side?

After the diagnosis and the onset of the disease, it took time to come to grips with all the changes the disease brought to both my husband's and my life. I became sad and depressed. Then angry for the silence of my telephone and the lack of visitors in my home. It was the next year at an Easter communion service I finally came to grips with the forgiveness I needed to give and thus free my own soul.

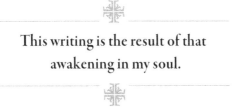

**This writing is the result of that
awakening in my soul.**

Pause for Reflection...

Has your social life been affected by the trials, tribulations, or traumas in your life?

THE CROSS

What did they look like from that lone and singular place? Did they look familiar? Were there people there with whom you have shared a drink, broken bread, and laughed together at a humorous story? Were some of them people whom you expected to be there for you, champion your teachings, and offering sorrowing support when this time came? You did try to prepare them for this event. You told them it was coming. They did not understand. They had traveled with you through some really hard times! The storms of living had beaten down on all of your faces. You had shared moments that you thought would seal them in loyalty to your friendship forever.

As you scanned the crowd, did you see their faces there, wanting to comfort you? Was their absence unbearably painful? The scoffers, the ones for whom you held no expectations, took center stage. They had beaten your body, stolen your clothes, and mocked your name. They did not know who you were, but where were your friends? Where were the ones who did know you? Those other people made a scene, but where were your defenders? Was there no one to be counted on? How did you bear their absence? How did you bear their silence when no one came to your defense in your waiting silence? Perhaps, the worst people at that place were not the ones who did not know you, but the ones who did, and never offered comfort!

Yet, I heard you offer forgiveness to those who did not know what they did to you. Was that forgiveness for your friends as well? Should they not have known better? I can understand forgiving ignorance, but those people who have shared your presence on holidays, as well as in the everyday activities, are they not more accountable for their hiding silence?

I know what it feels like, Lord, to have your friends not show up in deep sorrow. I believed if my time ever came, I would need a church family to support me, yes, even carry me for a while. I believed someone would be there! Actually, I could not imagine what such a time would feel like, but in my imaginings, I could not really know what that time would feel like. I do now!

Dreams shattered, a lifestyle lost, frightened for the future, the unknown, all became entangled in deep grief that could not be expressed. I felt so alone, even in the midst of a crowd of people. You, Lord, were also with a huge crowd of people. They were not your friends that day. If they were there, they were helpless as they stared at you on that cross.

"Father, forgive them," You said.

I would have stood there in silence, too, wouldn't I? I would have failed You, as well. Help me to forgive them, Lord. I needed those friends to comfort me, but they did not understand my loss. I could not speak. I felt embalmed! Oh, Lord, You died that day on the cross for all our sins and weaknesses. You offered forgiveness before each of us knew we needed forgiveness. Heal my soul. Let me offer forgiveness, even before anyone knows what their silence has destroyed in me, what barriers I have now erected, and what faith has been diminished. Help me tear down all that stands between You and me, and the others, as well! Father, forgive them; they do not know what they have done! You were the most alone person in the whole world. You do understand, Lord. Help me to forgive as well!

It has been a while since I wrote this. However, the challenge to stay connected is an ongoing activity that requires diligence that can be easily discouraged by the difficult days of sickness and isolation that the disease thrusts into one's life. The caretaker becomes part of the scenario and depression is an ever-threatening enemy. Denny's Parkinson's often caused him to sleep restlessly or not at all. Those are the nights I found the most difficult as exhaustion can sneak up on you and one does not realize what is wrong.

After a particularly difficult week of sleeplessness, I went to the little local grocery to purchase a few necessary items. I fell asleep in front of the soup aisle, resting on the handle of the grocery cart. A kind gentleman asked me if I was all right. It is difficult to explain what one needs during these times.

Expectations may be unreasonable, but if one asks me, I just say, "Show up!" You cannot fix it or make it go away. Let others know that you care for them.

A cut rose from your garden, a favorite bag of cookies, and a good book you have read are all a few suggestions of ice breakers when entering an environment where you are not sure what to say. A hug says a lot!

I recently called a dear friend whose husband is in the advanced stages of Alzheimer' Disease. She was expressing to me the loss of many friendships as her husband becomes less communicative. She was particularly hurt by not receiving an invitation to a going-away party for a mutual friend of the party hostess. She said she had just heard about the party that was held last week and inquired as to why she wasn't invited.

The hostess was surprised by the question and answered, "I only had ten chairs."

My friend cried, "I was the eleventh chair!"

Pause for Reflection...

Will you choose to forgive those who were not able to stand with you through these trying circumstances?

TOWN CELEBRATIONS

The Allensville Festival was the biggest celebration in town for the year. It was an annual event as a fundraiser for the fire company. When I was young, my grandfather, and then my Dad would always run the kewpie doll stand. There were dolls on sticks and balls to bounce, feathered fans, and velvet dice to hang on your car mirror. I loved throwing nickels onto plates and vases to win said object. There was a live mouse game, where it was dumped into the center of a rotating table and whatever numbered hole he disappeared into was the winner. There were darts to throw at balloons for a win. There were balls to be thrown at stacked bowling pins. If one was lucky, someone would bring a pony and one could pay for a ride around the park grounds. One could smell the chicken corn soup, fried hamburgers, and hot dogs with chili, sauerkraut or onions all over town for two glorious days. There were slices of delicious apple, cherry, lemon custard, raisin, and sho-fly pies. There were always half-moon pies and whoopie pies.

Funnel cake stands were a must, while French fries were always popular as well.

It was during one of these days of preparing for the festival that my friend, Carol, and I got into another frustrating event for her mother. Goldie was baking three cherry pies for the festival. We begged her for a taste of the cherries.

She said she wanted the pies to be full of cherries, so she answered, "No, go and play!"

After a time of being outside, we came back onto the summer porch, glassed enclosed, and saw the pies cooling from the oven. One of us decided we could just poke a small hole in the pie and taste the now-warm cherries. They were not only warm; they were still not gelled. When the pie was tipped on its side the cherries ran out of the shell. We ate all three cherry fillings and left the pie shells. I headed for home immediately! I knew we were in big trouble. Both mothers ended up baking pies way into the night, while I missed the first night of the festival!

Pause for Reflection...

Do you attend local community events and support those who serve your community?

If there are no such events, contact your local Chamber of Commerce and see if you help organize one. It will bring the people in your community together for fun and fellowship.

HOLIDAYS

My parents loved to celebrate the holidays! My two brothers and I were always the center of their celebrations. On Easter, our baskets were found after a long trail of crepe paper ribbon was attached to our beds and threaded throughout the house to the hidden basket. ST. Patrick's Day was a real reason to turn everything in the house a shade of green. Green water, green eggs and ham, and at dinner time mashed potatoes became a shade of green. My mother was Irish and named Kathleen. My Dad was forever singing songs with Kathleen as a prominent word in the melody. We all dressed in green on that day of celebration. I still do!

Valentine's Day was filled with homemade valentines and sweet treats. Most everything found on this day was red or pink in color. I carried the celebrations I was taught into my marriage. Denny's family did not celebrate these events. He did not have a birthday cake until we were dating, and I baked him one. One Valentine's Day he came home from work and stared at the red and pink dining room table with hearts everywhere and quickly tried to leave. I stopped him at the door and told him he was too late to buy a gift.

"The children now already know you forgot Valentine's Day."

He never forgot another one!

Christmas was a different day of celebration. It had a spiritual emphasis which we held sacred. We had birthday cakes to honor Jesus' birth. We exchanged gifts, but they were not the center of the day. The day was all about family and fellowship. We did have large meals of food always shared at Christmas with aunts, uncles, cousins, and grandparents. I was so blessed to know them! Attending church was a part of what we did to honor His birth; hoping all the while to keep Christ in Christmas.

Summer celebrations were always a reason for a picnic. We would go at a moment's notice. If one has cheese, crackers, bread, and mustard, add a can of sardines or mini canned sausages and off you go! The kids all preferred hot dogs, but the adults had a finer palate! We did not need a picnic table to eat, a blanket on the ground by a stream would do. All the better for a stream, which meant we could go wading and catch tadpoles.

Memorial celebrations often involved a parade. We were taught at an earlier age to respect the military and often laid flowers on those loved ones who were in the cemetery.

Did your family celebrate various
holidays together?

If that was not a family tradition, why not
initiate such celebrations in the coming
year. Such times bring families together
and give the next generation
wonderful memories.

THE BUCKET LIST

Denny wanted to visit all of the United States before he died. I wanted to make that happen. We had been traveling with a timeshare vacation for over twenty years. I was one who loved to travel anywhere that was new and interesting. Denny preferred home if given a choice! When he did travel, he wanted it to be in the United States. I wanted to see the world! We did some compromising. When he was diagnosed with Parkinson's, he only had ten states he had not visited. After ten years, he only had six states and they were mostly found in the northern border of the United States. I asked a couple who were friends if they would like to go with us. They said yes! I spent a year planning the six-week trip. We purchased a travel van. It had better glide seating and a special comfort ride insert in the construction of the vehicle.

We all charged everything to a special credit card that gave us free nights for each dollar amount spent. One has to keep track of this amount monthly and pay it off each month for this to work. After a year, each couple had saved enough to get three weeks of free hotels with a breakfast included. We mostly packed our lunches and ate one meal a day at local restaurants.

One week, we spent at a timeshare in the mid-west USA. It was a glorious time. We traveled the whole way to the West Coast and stopped at all the National Parks along the way. The unexpected was normal with a visit to a farm for rescued injured bears—two hundred on roaming range. There was a man who started a farm for prairie-dogs. The problem was they kept escaping by digging under the fence! We discovered a hidden coastline of giant redwood trees when my friend had to do a quick and necessary potty stop in California. The strawberries were so large in Oregon, a single berry-filled the palm of my hand! I could go on and on, but please sometime go and see it all for yourself. The United States is amazing.

When telling Denny's doctor about the planned trip, he was not excited about it. He looked at me and asked me if I understood how ill Denny was? We left his office discouraged. That evening he called me and said he had been thinking about our trip and realized that when Denny came to see him, he never talked about his disease. Instead, he spent the time telling him where he had been and what he had seen. Perhaps for Denny, this trip would be continued treatment, after all, we could always turn around.

We finished his bucket list with several years to spare.

Pause for Reflection...

Write out your bucket list and do not wait
too long to begin to fulfill it.

THE DANCE

My man was a dancing fool. If one could learn a new dance and do it, he would! I learned that when I was just fifteen and he was sixteen. He would coax me on to the school dance floor while gyrating to the latest music. I loved to dance with him!

At our forty-fourth anniversary we talked about how to celebrate our fiftieth anniversary.

Denny said, "Honey, I doubt if I will be able to dance five years from now. My legs are already stiff."

I thought about that for a while and suggested we should celebrate with friends that next year!

**We deserved it
and it was a good way to
carry on with no regrets!
He agreed.**

We invited our network of friends we'd made through the years. They came from all over the U.S.A. It was wonderful! Even my friend, Carol, from the childhood days of mayhem, came with her husband. Our DJ played songs from our past and introduced some from the present. Ten of our eleven grandkids made it to the celebration. Denny's and my children did a comedy routine by lining up like the Rockettes and reciting, "Everything we ever learned in life we learned growing up in jail." They then individually told their jail-time stories. It was a different way to raise a family. Denny and I danced the day away in each other's arms, while I held onto him fervently.

He asked, "Do you love me now?"

I said, "From a long time before and forever!"

Pause for Reflection...

Remember to celebrate your love for one another and your family. That way there will be no regrets!

It Is a Long Journey...

It is two A.M. and Denny has just taken his first of two nighttime medications. He often sleeps through the whole administration of these meds. After ten years of taking multiple drugs, the side effects are still unpredictable. He needs them to control his Parkinson's symptoms, yet they also sometimes cause confusion, sleepwalking, restlessness, and never-remembered conversations with past or present acquaintances. It has been over ten years since Denny's first doctor's visit that declared the Parkinson's Disease that now is part of his life.

The journey, as we were always told, would be progressive. Progressive sounds like a good word until one uses it with a debilitating illness. The losses are slow, yet one day there they are! Denny can no longer drive a car, write a check to pay a bill or hold a small grandchild without the worry of inadvertently tossing them with an uncontrolled arm jerk. The constant loss of hot and cold drinks tossed in the air is a given! I often lose precious sleep nurturing Denny back into sleep while becoming wide awake myself. Days and nights seem like one, only divided by light and darkness. This loss of sleep is the most difficult side effect I experience as a caretaker.

Some days, I feel like my role as Denny's wife has been swapped out for nurse, director of activities, and chauffeur to scheduled appointments. It is a big emotional loss as all the other roles are essential to our existence. However, here I am, sitting in a lovely resort bedroom on Hilton Head, SC Island, listening to the waves roll in from the ocean to the sandy shore.

The ocean sounds remind me that some things
really are meant to be ongoing
such as the ocean returning its waters
back to land on a heaven-scheduled return.

Depression is the biggest enemy we both face as the losses become more evident. Not only are they more evident, but one knows with a "progressive disease" there are more changes coming. Although I continue to travel as much as Denny can tolerate, traveling is now much contained. I would not complain as we have had some wonderful travels in these last ten years. I continue to live with the mantra of living with "No Regrets." It doesn't always work!

I usually at this point can deliver a much rosier comment. Today, I am tired and spent and filled with some sadness for what might have been. I usually do not write on days I feel like this. Without these pages, though, this book would not be complete! I can continue to say that without the Lord in my life the situation would be intolerable and destroying.

The Lord is my strength, my shield, and He continues to walk through the fire with Denny and me.

There is always tomorrow, and although the situation will not change, there will be changes to the situation. There will be days of more sleep, visits or calls from friends who care, a good, near pain-free day for Denny or just a day with me having a better attitude. This has become our lives.

Someone who loves me asked once what did I miss most in the losses? At the time, I said quickly Denny being able to hold me at night without his diseased body pushing me away in jerking tremors! But now, I have mostly adjusted to even that! I just hold on! No, my biggest fear is that I will forget in the mayhem all the small sweet memories I have collected over the disease-free years of our marriage! The first birthdays of each of our children, their wedding days; the new face of a crying grandchild as my child delivered her from her body. The simplicity of tender lovemaking or watching Denny trim and fuss over his rose bushes. Most of his gardening days are over! However, I say once more, today, as the new dawn now bursts over the ocean waves and onto the sandy shores of Hilton Head, we have had an incredible life already lived. I think of the scripture that always perplexed me until I needed to live it!

"Who am I to say to my maker why have you made me thus and so?" (Romans 9:20-21).

Today, I am Yours to do with as You wish, Lord. Praise Your holy name!

Love,
Susan

Pause for Reflection...

As each new day dawns, can you also say, "Today, I am Yours to do with as You wish, Lord. Praise Your holy name!"

Our Family Circle – A Letter to My Children

In my life, the family is the glue that holds my earthly world together. Our circle began on the day Denny and I married. Through words of commitments and promises before God, we established the foundation of our family. Each new life God added to our family for care and guidance brought another personality, new joys, new problems, and an incredible, deeper love. I could not imagine after having the first child that I would be able to love another as much as I loved this child already filling my heart with an all-encompassing love. However, with each new person added to the family, my love stretched like a colorful rubber balloon.

Each person, when added to the other,
made us more complete,
serving the whole and, thus,
becoming family.

As parents, our role becomes different from the children who make up the family. We nurture and feed their bodies and souls. Our lives are intertwined forever with their lives, though the ultimate goal is to prepare them to leave and establish their own families. Our goal is to lead them to a higher guidance than ours, to know and serve the Lord!

It is difficult to explain, but so easy to feel how important the solidarity of this family has become to both Denny and me. Each child has now selected a mate to form their own family and new babies are added in a fusion of love. Our family circle has now been enlarged and also asked to accept even more personalities, more joys, more problems, and an even deeper love. It might be more difficult for the siblings in these family relationships to always see themselves as part of the whole as they do go on and form their own families.

For Denny and me, we only see this once small family of love that began with our marriage vows and now has exploded into a family that fills us with pride, joy, laughter, and sometimes tears. What we are is a family. In you, my family, I have all my hopes, all my dreams, and a legacy that will continue when I am no longer a part of this earth. We are now a part of the family circle just as I also was once the hope and future of the family that went before me. We are family! You are loved!

Mother

Pause for Reflection...

Always remember, our goal is to lead our families to a higher guidance than ours as they come to know and serve the Lord!

A Proud American!

We traveled as often as Denny was able to enjoy the schedule of the trip. It was on one of these trips that I met a special man staring into the rearview mirror of his tour bus. He was a driver for the tour company that was escorting my husband and me around Los Angeles. I cannot say that he impressed me, particularly as I got on the bus. He was quiet and observed each of us on the bus from the rearview mirror. I noticed his eyes which searched our individual faces and I remember thinking, "I wonder what he is thinking as he looks at us?"

It is easy to ignore someone who is driving the bus from one place to another. In this case, he was picking several of us up at Disneyland and dropping us off at our hotels. We were tired from a full day at the park. The evening had gotten cooler and the bus was warm. My husband and I were scheduled to be the last tourists delivered to the hotel for the evening. In the silence, after the second to last persons were dropped off at their hotel, he began a conversation by asking us where we lived. I told him Central

Pennsylvania. He asked how long we were visiting the area. This was a general "chit-chat" that we were used to, as this was our third week away from home.

What became different was the change in his voice as he told us that he had just gotten back from a three-month visit to Ethiopia. He proceeded to tell us that he was a native of that country. He came here to attend school and had become a soccer player of some renown. He had traveled all over the country with his soccer team. He said he had injured his knee and thus was forced to find other employment. He was now retired and did this job to raise money to take supplies back to Ethiopia. I was mesmerized by the lilting accent his voice had as he continued to tell us his life story.

He became a U.S. citizen, had married, and now had two married daughters and five grandchildren. His wife was a registered nurse, as well as both of his daughters. He told us with a now, emotion-filled voice, how blessed he was to be able to live as a free man with his family in this wonderful free nation. He said there was such poverty in his birth nation that he could not forget where he came from and the great needs that existed there today. Therefore, he was spending his retirement in appeals to all kinds of organizations from food banks to dentists and physicians to give their wears and skills as he did, as donations to his beloved Ethiopia.

He said he particularly revered education as a means to a way out of the extreme situation of poverty and tyranny that existed there today. He spent his time educating the people on how to make better choices with their lives and gave whatever skills and supplies he had to make those changes happen. He told us how fortunate we were to be born in this free, affluent nation.

I was impressed with his deep love for my country and the reverence in his voice when he mentioned her name. I thought how privileged I was to be reminded again of what a great country we have that allows all peoples to find refuge and strength in her borders. Do I take for granted what gifts were mine at birth because someone went before me making those gifts possible?

As I reflected on his words, his eyes caught mine in the mirror. They were bright with determination as he declared he was the most grateful of all men, each night as he climbed into bed, no matter what exhaustion the day had brought, to sleep under the nation of the United States.

I had once more been reminded that freedom really never was free.

It has been a gift from those who have paid the price for its existence.

One man took the time one night to tell me his story; a story I think that has become his mission of love to share!

Pause for Reflection...

Ask yourself, do I take for granted
what gifts were mine at birth because
someone went before me making those
gifts possible?

Remember to honor them!

The Rescue!

The day was stone grey, and the sun could not decide if it wanted to shine or hide. It had been a long cold winter and I was anxious to get out of the house for a planned escape from the winter "blahs." I had called my friend, Judy, to see if she and her son were interested in accompanying me on a day-long shopping trip. My daughter, Carrie, and Judy's son, Greg, were both four years old and were already great playmates. They were well-behaved children, who listened to their mothers, and in the past had been easy to manage while we were shopping.

Despite the weather, I was looking forward to the day. Just as I was putting on my coat, I had this feeling which felt almost like a friend talking to me, saying, "Do not go over the mountain; go the long way around the mountain." I thought to myself, if I take the road around the mountain, we will not have very long to shop before we will have to come home to meet my older children's school bus. I then decided to continue with my plans for the shorter jaunt over the mountain.

I quickly placed Carrie in the station wagon. She scampered to her favorite, facing back, the third seat to wait for Greg to arrive. As I looked into the distance, Judy was coming down the highway. She honked her car horn in enthusiastic anticipation of a fun-filled day. Just as she got out of her car, I once more heard the same warning, "Do not go over the mountain; go the long way around the mountain." I thought that I was just being nervous; the winter had been harsh and had provoked a lot of difficult driving experiences. I headed off to take the short cut over the mountain. I thought about telling Judy what I had experienced in hearing and feeling the warning, but it seemed too silly to mention.

The clouds parted and the sun began to shine. I looked up the mountain road and inwardly laughed at my hearing those strange "warning voices" in my head. The road looked snow and ice-free as the warm sun reflected off the blacktop surface. My friend, Judy, and I were talking about our recent Bible study on the study of angels and their roles in our lives. It was a new topic for us. We were both doing a lot of scripture reading and locating places in the Bible that mentioned angels being a part of people's lives. The children were entertaining themselves in the back seat.

As I approached the top of the mountain, suddenly the car hit a patch of dark, thick ice on the road. The car spun out of control and into a metal guardrail, which was the only thing that was keeping the car from spiraling down the deep mountainside. I crawled over the seats to the back of the car and looked down over the mountain. The restraining guardrail was bulging. I then tried to get out of the car to access the damage. When my feet hit the ice, I slid under the car. I had to hold onto my friend's outstretched hand and the underframe of the car to pull myself back into the vehicle. The road had had cinders placed on it, but they had melted onto the road and refrozen into black ice during the cold March night.

The children were crying with fear, as they peered out their back window and down the mountain. I then admitted to my friend that I had this feeling that I was not supposed to go this way, twice. I also admitted that I had never had a similar experience, so I ignored it! I had not told anyone where I was going. I expected to be home before anyone else in the family. We tried calming the children by singing a little song.

We then did what we should have done right away and began to pray. I told the Lord how foolish I was and realized He had tried to warn me with His Spirit. I also asked Him to rescue us. The children calmed down as if waiting to be saved. For the situation Judy and I were in, we were surprisingly calm. I believed if I was warned several times not to go up on the mountain road, and indeed was now on that mountain road, that the Lord knew where I was now stranded.

My deafness to His warnings was also my foolishness!

A short period of time passed, then we heard the sound of a rattling vehicle coming up the other side of the mountain. We watched the top of the mountain road as an old, paint speckled pickup truck with tools hanging off a rack mounted on the bed of the truck, came over the crest of the road. The tools jangled as the driver drove to a halt opposite my car. The man was rather old, with bib overalls, several days' growth of beard on his face, and chewing an unlit cigar. He got out of the truck and walked to the center of the road. It was the same road that I was unable to stand on just a short time ago.

I said, "I need help. Can you help me?"

He said, "You sure were foolish for coming up on this mountain!"

I admitted that I was foolish. I also looked at Judy, wondering what she was thinking at all that was happening.

She shrugged her shoulders and said, "We did pray for help. Do you think he is an angel?"

I never imagined that an angel looked like this man. The cigar was an unlikely accessory. However, he was standing on slick, smooth ice giving me a mini-lecture on my foolishness! He then asked me if I trusted him.

I once more looked at Judy and said, "I think the Lord has answered our prayers by sending this person, perhaps he is an angel."

She concurred. I told him I did trust him.

He said, "Will you do whatever I tell you to do?"

I shook my head in the affirmative. He then moved a little closer to the center of the road and posed to give directions.

He removed the chewed cigar from his mouth and began to speak.

"Start your car, turn your wheel slowly to the right—now to the left—and back again."

The car slowly started to move onto the center of the road.

He then loudly yelled, "Brake!"

I slammed my foot onto the brake and the big station wagon did a U-turn back down the hill as I steered it like a sled for several minutes onto the dry road. I pulled over to the side of the road. My hands were shaking uncontrollably, and I needed to take a deep breath! I wanted to wait and thank the man for his help in getting us off the mountain. His truck had been directly across from us on the road and was headed in our direction down the mountain. We waited for twenty minutes. He never came down the mountain.

I looked at Judy and she stared at me. For several minutes we did not say anything to each other. We were surprisingly quiet as we returned home. We knew we had been rescued from a mountain peril. Occasionally, we still talk about the time we might have met an angel on the icy mountain. I cannot tell you for sure if that old man was an angel, but I now listen when I hear those voices giving me intuitive messages that might protect me and the ones I love.

I also think God has a terrific sense of humor, perhaps, sending His angels in forms of persons that the ordinary day and circumstance might just ignore.

Pause for Reflection...

Learn from my mistake and make sure you
listen to that still small voice of the Holy
Spirit as He gives you intuitive messages
from your loving heavenly Father.

Final Word

I hope all of you who have chosen to read my book are blessed by its reading. I am blessed to have this manuscript go to print. Everyone has a story tell. I pray this book has inspired you to tell your story. May God go with you!

Dennis Reed Erhard
Homegoing, October 23, 2015

Do you know my Savior?

I have been writing this book for over twenty years. It is the story of how God, my Savior, has been growing me into the woman He has created me to be. He knew me before I was born in my mother's womb (Ps. 139). He called me when I was just a child, and He saved me for eternity to be with Him. Many of my stories reflect how He met me at different places in my life. He loved me with His comfort and guidance. You can also have this relationship with Jesus. (Psalm 71:18-18.)

I invite you to pray this prayer: "Lord Jesus Christ, I repent of my sins. Thank you for dying for me and for your shed blood in the forgiveness of my sin. I surrender to you as my personal Lord and Savior. Thank you for giving me eternal life, Amen."

About the Author

Susan Updegrove Erhard. I been writing since I was just a young girl. I have submitted stories to writing contests in the local, home publications. I have won a few contests, but the thrill of writing was enough to keep me going. I have a degree in nursing but spent most of my life owning and running my own antique, gift and décor stores. I have served in the administration of local women clubs in all positions while becoming a speaker in that arena. I continue to teach Bible studies as opportunities arise. I also have led several weekend retreats on women in the Bible. I am the mother of four children and eleven grandchildren. I was married to my high school sweetheart for fifty years. We raised our family while basically living on prison properties as my husband was the warden of Pennsylvania state prisons. We both grew up in Big Valley located in the Kishacoquillas Valley in central Pennsylvania. A beautiful place to live. Currently, I also reside in Mechanicsburg, PA.